Chocolate Affirmations

LEAH LOVE

ARCHWAY
PUBLISHING

Archway Publishing books may be ordered through booksellers or by contacting:

Archway Publishing
1663 Liberty Drive
Bloomington, IN 47403
www.archwaypublishing.com
844-669-3957

ISBN: 978-1-6657-2665-8 (sc)
ISBN: 978-1-6657-2666-5 (e)

Library of Congress Control Number: 2022942155

Print information available on the last page.

Archway Publishing rev. date: 10/31/2022

To all the courageous, powerful, and brave women in my life. I have learned from you, and I have watched you. This book is in honor of you and your power. Thank you for showing me my strength.

Contents

Introduction

I finally found the courage to write down my thoughts. I finally found the freedom to share my heart with the world. My experiences, my hopes, and my dreams coat these pages from top to bottom. I hope these words speak to those who read them. I hope this compilation of thoughts gives inspiration to those who need it.

May the love inside fill you with peace. May my truth open your mind. May this book break down barriers and walls that have been built over a lifetime. May these words shatter any negative thoughts you ever had about yourself, your past, and your present.

I wish you all the love and light the world has to offer.

Forever yours.

The Beginning

The world does not really want you
in your raw, God-given form.
To be loved and indulged,
you need to become a modified version of yourself.
The world prefers you sweeter, lighter, processed, put together
but that is not you.

That is not who you are.

You are raw.
You are real.
You are undone.

It is time for the world to see you for who you really are.

It is time for the world to know what you are really made of.

–Chocolate Affirmations

When you look at me, what do you see?
Do you see hopes, dreams, and potential?
Do you see wealth, abundance, and joy?
When you look at me, do you see beauty?
Do you see a well-educated woman?
Do you see someone who will make a difference in the world
and change it for the better?
Ask yourself when you look at me, what do you see?
More importantly, what do you feel?
When I look at me, I will tell you exactly what I see.
When I look at me, I see that my nose is crooked when I
smile. I see my uneven skin tone; I see my blemishes, my
pores, and my scars. I see that my teeth could be whiter.
When I look in the mirror, I see everything you see and
beyond. I am my own skeptic, critic, and everything in
between.

However, while I see these imperfections in myself, I also
strive to see my glory.

–Internal Thoughts

I see my strength on days when I have none.
I see my motivation when it is often invisible.
I see and feel everything that makes me whole.
I see my gratitude for life, my determination to live,
my gumption to go for my goals, and my grit to keep going.
I see my crown is tilted every single day,
but the moment my feet touch the ground, that is my cue to adjust it.
The world waits for no one; time is always of the essence.
I have realized that what you see when you look at me does not
really matter.

I am who I am.
I will be who I will be.
I am beautiful.
I am her.
I am she.
I am me.

—Reflections

Questions

What are you made of?
Merely man and woman,
Or is it more?
Are you made of the earth, the sky, and the sea?
The motherland?
Is it cinnamon, pepper, or clove?
Spice?
Are you made of leather, bondage, and bones?
Slavery?
Is it new age, funk, or soul?
Culture?
Is it blood, sweat, and tears?
Talent?
Are you made of caramel, toffee, and butter?
Dessert?
Or is it bullets, bombs, and shells?
Violence?
Are you soft, warm, and just like home?
Comfort?
Are you hard and cold?
Armor?
Do you really have a place to call your own?
Besides your wounds,
Your scars,
Your hair,
Your heart,
Or was that taken from you too?
What do you really have to call your own?

—A Message from Your Ancestors

Has anyone ever told you about the magic in your pigment?

–The Foundation of It All

You stand for it, but does it stand for you?

–The Flag

Why does my beauty cause you so much devastation?

–Racism

Why are you hiding your true self from the world?

–Insecurities

What would they say if they knew how you really felt?

–Facade

Why do we reveal and hide simultaneously?

–Exposure

Recollections

To limit your potential.

–Withhold

To speak without bounds.

–Truth

To go back to that place you once promised you would not.

–The Past

To lose the battle with yourself.

–Addiction

The deepest part of the soul.

–Love

To draw a line in the sand.

–Boundaries

To see without sight.

–Vision

To have something once lost.

–Treasure

The message we tell ourselves when we look in the mirror.

–Never Enough

Letters

Dear Little One,

If you are reading this, just know I love you. Be a good little girl for your mother and father. Be a loving sister and cherish your memories always. You will never get them back, and you will replay them in your head every day of your life.

Do not be offended when people stare at you or ask you about your hair. Do everything you can to educate them about it with confidence and love! Always love your hair. God has certainly blessed you with enough of it!

I want you to love your complexion. God chose your shade of chocolate especially for you, and no one else in the world has its particular blend.

The little boys only make fun of you because they are jealous. You are smarter and faster than all of them. The little girls tease you at recess because they want what you have. They have never seen anything like you, and they never will.

Be brave. Be strong. Have fun and enjoy every moment of your life before you grow up. No matter what, please do not grow up too fast. Life is so beautiful, but it does get hard. Do not ever let the world taint your sweet spirit.

Love Always,

–Your Older Self

Dearest Young Woman,

Everyone you love in your life is going to hurt you, but especially the ones who were never capable of loving you at all. You will go through times when you feel unstoppable. You will also go through times when you feel completely and utterly powerless. You must come to a point when you must save yourself from yourself. It is true what they say: You must love yourself before you can truly love anyone else.

Do not believe them when they say you cannot win. Do not believe them when they say your dreams are too big. People want you to believe in their own failures. Do not force anything, be it a job, an opportunity, or love. Everything will happen the way it should.

You must learn to recognize a blessing in disguise. Many doors will close for you so that better ones will open. As much as you want to jump out of that window ... don't!

You will eventually find a path that is clear. You suffer because you choose to see all the love and beauty in the world. For that you will be punished. Please realize it is only a test of your love, your gifts, and your talents. You will be tested often. It will all make sense one day. I promise.

Until that day comes, do not be still; embrace everything that makes you bright. Do not let the world dull your shine. And no matter what you do, remain true to yourself and the person God created you to become.

–Your Oldest Self

Dearest Daughter,

How do I even begin to describe my love for you? You will never understand the love between a mother and her daughter until you have children of your own someday. When you were born, I cried so many tears of joy, but I also cried tears of sadness. I want to do everything in my power to protect you from any harm that may ever come your way. I see you and your beauty, and all I can think of is how can I protect her from getting hurt? How can I prepare her for the world, from getting her heart broken, from betrayal?

Even before you were born, it was like I could feel your heart beating in my body. I tried my best to prepare a perfect home for you for nine months. I knew the moment you took your first breath of fresh air that my troubles and my greatest hopes would all become real.

The world is going to try to push you to become so many things. It may be an athlete, a model, a scholar, an artist, a singer, an engineer, or nothing at all. Just know the world is yours. You can become anything and anyone you choose to become. Do not succumb to the pressures of society. You must make your own choices about your life, your body, your love, and your future.

My greatest wish is for you to become a woman who, above all else, loves and respects her family, herself, her culture, and every individual walking the planet. May you possess humility, dignity, and confidence. Do not forget you are a descendant of royalty, and you, my dear, will inherit the kingdom one day.

–Your Loving Mother

Dearest Son,

I am so proud to call you my son. You are so precious, so innocent, and so perfect. Unfortunately, the world will not always see you in that light. One day, when you are old enough to run, the world will see you as a threat. You will no longer be cute; instead, you will be perceived as dangerous. Your father and I will have conversations with you about how to speak and act around the police. We will have to show you where to place your hands. We will tell you what volume and tone to speak at when spoken to by an officer.

We will even have conversations about what you wear. The world has had a specific perception about you from the moment you are born. You will feel trapped in your skin, your body, and your mind. You will never feel free. We will do our best to shatter the shackles, the burden of fear, and the institutional racism you may face every day of your life.

Remember this: At home you will always be a king. You will always be allowed to sit at the head of the table, no questions asked. Please know how loved you are. To us, you are royalty always and forever. But please know the world will never agree. They will only agree if you become rich and famous and powerful, a professional athlete, and so on and so forth. You are worthy of the greatest love and success the world has to offer. Never forget that. You are already enough.

–Your Loving Mother

Dearest Mom,

If it were not for you, I would never know the meaning of love. You have given me enough of it to last a lifetime. Your hugs, your support, your kindness, they are all things I will never forget. You are the reason I am the woman I am today. I now understand why you were so protective of me throughout my life. I realize how much you have done for me and all the sacrifices you have made. I understand everything now.

My heart is an extension of your own. I know you have always felt it was your greatest honor to keep it safe from harm. I love to see you happy, but I hate seeing you worry. You never really told me that life was short and to make the most of it. You were afraid of giving me advice you, too, did not know how to follow. You have been there to listen during my anger, my frustration, and my pain. You were there when I needed a shoulder to cry on and when I needed someone to wipe my messy tears. You have always been there, and you always will be, until one day when you will not.

Please know the day I lose you will be the worst day of my life. Your love has been the greatest gift I have known, and it is an honor to have it.

If I can be half the mom you are someday, I will be content with that.

–Your Daughter, Your Heart

Dear Sister,

I never knew I would have a best friend from the moment I was born. You have always been there to keep a watchful eye on me. You have always been there to spoil me and give me advice. I have always admired so much about you. You helped teach me so many important lessons in life without even knowing it.

You are my keeper. My keeper of secrets, my keeper of wishes, and my keeper of dreams. You have even been a lifesaver a time or two. I watch you as a mother, and it makes me so excited to have children of my own someday. I have seen you laugh, cry, and everything in between. You are a version of me, yet you are your own person.

I have always looked up to you, I have always wanted to be more like you. When I was young, I used to pray to God to make time pass quickly so I may grow older like you. You have always been my muse and my guardian angel at the same time.

You may not know, but you are an amazing teacher. I have certainly learned some of the best lessons from you.

–Love, Your Little Sister

My Hair

It is the true protector of my most sacred parts,
It is a way to measure my growth,
It is my self-expression,
It is my escape,
It shows no judgment towards me,
It challenges me,
It enhances me,
It is my security,
It is my gift to do whatever I please with,
It is mine to cherish,
It is mine to love,
It is one of the most important parts of me.

–My Hair

Why is it that my decision about my hair is so disruptive to your life?
Only when it grows upon your head,
should you be allowed to be concerned with it.
So much time is spent asking why I choose
to keep my hair the way I do.
I wish there were more honor and respect when it comes to my hair.
I did not have a part to play in how my hair grows from its follicles.
I had no part to play in my roots.
I had no part to play in its texture.
You act as if it were something you have never seen before in your life.
You act as if it was an unsolvable puzzle
Or an illogical mathematical equation.
Do I dare say you act as if it were from a different planet?

–Audacity

Just because something is different
does not mean it is any less beautiful.

–Humanity

When it comes to my hair,
let me tell you what I will allow.
I will allow admiration,
I will allow thought-provoking questions,
I will allow honor,
I will allow respect,
I will allow love,
I will allow acceptance,
I will welcome a genuine smile,
I will allow educated questions,
I will only accept the love you show for your own.

–Standard

Authenticity

There is more to me than looks.
I have a brain, abilities, and my own thoughts too.

–Thoughts of the Second Brain

I do not need your stamp of approval to be valid.

–Postage

The color of my skin does not make me exotic.
Nor do the places I have traveled to.

–Exploration

My past will never be a measurement of my worth.

–Lessons

I love finding happiness in the smallest things.

–Satisfaction

Feeling small stops me from growing too big.
The mind is a powerful thing.

–Ego

Why am I deserving when so many others are not?

–Grateful

Self-Love

Why do we not allow ourselves to rest when we are tired?
Your body is craving a break
Before you fall apart.
When will you recognize your needs are important?

–Overworked

I long for the day when the face in the mirror nods with acceptance.

–Approval

I stopped chasing perfection the day I realized there was no such thing.

–Deception

Did you know you hail from kings and queens?

–Royalty

When was the last time you said I love you to yourself?

—Proclamation

Placing value on your happiness is the bravest thing a woman can do.

—Selfless

Chocolate
Affirmations

There are not many things I know for sure.
My list of affirmations is strong, yet powerful,
Direct and true.
I have taken every single experience in my life,
And have chosen to learn from them,
To be better because of them,
To grow from them.
I encourage you to look at your past not with envy or rage,
But look at it with understanding and acceptance.
Look at it as if it were the best teacher you ever had.
In this short life, we must choose wisely.
Our survival depends on it,
Our friends, our families.
But most important,
Our souls.
So tell me, what are your affirmations for yourself and your life?
What are those definitive statements that you will carry with you
throughout the course of your days?

The time is always now; let me show you how.

I will not allow myself to be defeated by the world.
I will find the power to keep pushing through
even the deepest pain.

Each day we are writing our own stories.
Your story is one of the most important stories ever written.

There is so much power in your story; do not be afraid to share it.

You are beautiful.
You are strong.
You are capable.

Believe you can achieve anything you want in this world.

You are a wonder,
You are a mystery,
You hold the key to your dreams.

I believe in *you*.
Say this until it is true.

Your truth will set you free.

What is your affirmation?
What do you want to declare for yourself and for your life?

What is your truth?
What are your wants and wishes?

What have you been dying to tell the world?

What have you done to make the world a better place?

How do you set your intentions for the days to come?

Are you proud of yourself and the life you have made?

Have you healed from the wounds of your past?

It is time to fear no more.
It is time to write your own story.
It is time to spread your wings,
Explore new places,
Meet new people,
Cherish the memories you are creating,
Love the life you have,
Find beauty in every person you see.
And most importantly,
Accept your own.
We will only be as powerful as we allow ourselves to become.
It is time for you to give yourself permission to be enough.
It is time for you to give yourself permission to
Be … unstoppable.

−A Declaration to All Women

The End

Printed in the United States
by Baker & Taylor Publisher Services